Super Han

MW01538376

Phone Number Email Log

Calendar

Weekly Planner

Bonuses

Website Passwords Log

Personal Goals

Vacation Planning

Packing List

Party Planning

Christmas Day Planner

Grocery List

Notebook

Lined Pages

Notes

Grid Dots

Gift ideas with a personal touch

MariaLeona.com
Follow Us On Instagram
@ArtMariaLeona

Important Info

FAMILY NAME: ....
ADDRESS: ....
HOME PHONE: ....

IN AN EMERGENCY CALL:

PARENT 1
NAME: ....
WORK PHONE: ....
CELL PHONE: ....

PARENT 2
NAME: ....
WORK PHONE: ....
CELL PHONE: ....

CHILDREN'S NAMES

CHILDREN'S CELL PHONE NUMBERS

SCHOOL NAME(S)

SCHOOL PHONE NUMBERS

EXTENDED FAMILY

NEIGHBORS & FRIENDS

NOTES:

Phone Numbers - eMails

FAMILY

FRIENDS

FREQUENT PLAYDATES

NEIGHBORS

BABYSITTERS

SCHOOLS/DAYCARE

KIDS' AFTER-SCHOOL PROGRAMS

KIDS' FAVORITE ATTRACTIONS

SALONS

GYMS/CLUBS

RESTAURANTS

TAKE-OUT/DELIVERY

VET

GROOMER

Phone Numbers - eMails

CONTRACTORS

HANDYMAN

REPAIRS

CLEANING SERVICES

LAWN SERVICE

SNOW REMOVAL

GARBAGE PICKUP

RECYCLING PICKUP

DECORATOR

OTHER

NOTES:

Phone Numbers - eMails

CONTRACTORS

HANDYMAN

REPAIRS

CLEANING SERVICES

LAWN SERVICE

SNOW REMOVAL

GARBAGE PICKUP

RECYCLING PICKUP

DECORATOR

OTHER

NOTES:

January

Monthly Focus

Top Three Things

1 _____
2 _____
3 _____

Special Dates

_____ _____
_____ _____
_____ _____
_____ _____
_____ _____

Home Keeping Tasks

☐ _____
☐ _____
☐ _____
☐ _____
☐ _____
☐ _____
☐ _____

Goals for the Month

_____ ☐
_____ ☐
_____ ☐
_____ ☐
_____ ☐
_____ ☐

_____ ☐
_____ ☐
_____ ☐
_____ ☐
_____ ☐
_____ ☐

_____ ☐
_____ ☐
_____ ☐
_____ ☐
_____ ☐
_____ ☐

Notes

_____
_____
_____
_____
_____
_____
_____
_____
_____
_____
_____
_____
_____
_____
_____
_____
_____
_____
_____
_____
_____
_____
_____
_____
_____

February

Monthly Focus

1 _____
2 _____
3 _____

Special Dates

_____ _____
_____ _____
_____ _____
_____ _____
_____ _____

Home Keeping Tasks

☐ _____
☐ _____
☐ _____
☐ _____
☐ _____
☐ _____
☐ _____

Goals for the Month

_____ ☐
_____ ☐
_____ ☐
_____ ☐
_____ ☐
_____ ☐

_____ ☐
_____ ☐
_____ ☐
_____ ☐
_____ ☐
_____ ☐

_____ ☐
_____ ☐
_____ ☐
_____ ☐
_____ ☐
_____ ☐

Notes

March

Monthly Focus

Top Three Things

1 _____
2 _____
3 _____

Special Dates

_____ _____
_____ _____
_____ _____
_____ _____
_____ _____

Home Keeping Tasks

- [ ] _____
- [ ] _____
- [ ] _____
- [ ] _____
- [ ] _____
- [ ] _____
- [ ] _____

Goals for the Month

_____ [ ]
_____ [ ]
_____ [ ]
_____ [ ]
_____ [ ]
_____ [ ]

_____ [ ]
_____ [ ]
_____ [ ]
_____ [ ]
_____ [ ]
_____ [ ]

_____ [ ]
_____ [ ]
_____ [ ]
_____ [ ]
_____ [ ]
_____ [ ]

Notes

_____
_____
_____
_____
_____
_____
_____
_____
_____
_____
_____
_____
_____
_____
_____
_____
_____
_____
_____
_____
_____
_____
_____
_____

April

Monthly Focus

Top Three Things

1 _____
2 _____
3 _____

Special Dates

___ _____
___ _____
___ _____
___ _____
___ _____
___ _____

Home Keeping Tasks

☐ _____
☐ _____
☐ _____
☐ _____
☐ _____
☐ _____
☐ _____

Goals for the Month

_____ ☐
_____ ☐
_____ ☐
_____ ☐
_____ ☐
_____ ☐

_____ ☐
_____ ☐
_____ ☐
_____ ☐
_____ ☐
_____ ☐

_____ ☐
_____ ☐
_____ ☐
_____ ☐
_____ ☐
_____ ☐

Notes

May

Monthly Focus

1 _____
2 _____
3 _____

Special Dates

_____ _____
_____ _____
_____ _____
_____ _____
_____ _____

Home Keeping Tasks

☐ _____
☐ _____
☐ _____
☐ _____
☐ _____
☐ _____
☐ _____

Goals for the Month

_____ ☐
_____ ☐
_____ ☐
_____ ☐
_____ ☐
_____ ☐

_____ ☐
_____ ☐
_____ ☐
_____ ☐
_____ ☐
_____ ☐

_____ ☐
_____ ☐
_____ ☐
_____ ☐
_____ ☐
_____ ☐

Notes
_____
_____
_____
_____
_____
_____
_____
_____
_____
_____
_____
_____
_____
_____
_____
_____
_____
_____
_____
_____
_____
_____
_____
_____
_____
_____
_____

June

Monthly Focus

Top Three Things

1 _____
2 _____
3 _____

Special Dates

_____
_____
_____
_____
_____

Home Keeping Tasks

☐ _____
☐ _____
☐ _____
☐ _____
☐ _____
☐ _____
☐ _____

Goals for the Month

☐
☐
☐
☐
☐
☐

☐
☐
☐
☐
☐
☐

☐
☐
☐
☐
☐
☐

Notes

July

Monthly Focus

Top Three Things

1 _____
2 _____
3 _____

Special Dates

_____ _____
_____ _____
_____ _____
_____ _____
_____ _____

Home Keeping Tasks

☐ _____
☐ _____
☐ _____
☐ _____
☐ _____
☐ _____
☐ _____

Goals for the Month

_____ ☐
_____ ☐
_____ ☐
_____ ☐
_____ ☐
_____ ☐

_____ ☐
_____ ☐
_____ ☐
_____ ☐
_____ ☐
_____ ☐

_____ ☐
_____ ☐
_____ ☐
_____ ☐
_____ ☐
_____ ☐

Notes

_____
_____
_____
_____
_____
_____
_____
_____
_____
_____
_____
_____
_____
_____
_____
_____
_____
_____
_____
_____
_____
_____
_____
_____
_____
_____
_____

August

Monthly Focus

1 _____
2 _____
3 _____

Special Dates

_____ _____
_____ _____
_____ _____
_____ _____
_____ _____

Home Keeping Tasks

☐ _____
☐ _____
☐ _____
☐ _____
☐ _____
☐ _____
☐ _____

Goals for the Month

☐
☐
☐
☐
☐
☐

☐
☐
☐
☐
☐
☐

☐
☐
☐
☐
☐
☐

Notes

September

Monthly Focus

1 _____
2 _____
3 _____

Special Dates

_____ _____
_____ _____
_____ _____
_____ _____
_____ _____

Home Keeping Tasks

☐ _____
☐ _____
☐ _____
☐ _____
☐ _____
☐ _____
☐ _____

Goals for the Month

_____ ☐
_____ ☐
_____ ☐
_____ ☐
_____ ☐
_____ ☐

_____ ☐
_____ ☐
_____ ☐
_____ ☐
_____ ☐
_____ ☐

_____ ☐
_____ ☐
_____ ☐
_____ ☐
_____ ☐
_____ ☐

Notes

_____
_____
_____
_____
_____
_____
_____
_____
_____
_____
_____
_____
_____
_____
_____
_____
_____
_____
_____
_____
_____
_____
_____
_____
_____
_____
_____
_____

October

Monthly Focus

Top Three Things

1 _____
2 _____
3 _____

Special Dates

_____ _____
_____ _____
_____ _____
_____ _____
_____ _____

Home Keeping Tasks

☐ _____
☐ _____
☐ _____
☐ _____
☐ _____
☐ _____
☐ _____

Goals for the Month

_____ ☐
_____ ☐
_____ ☐
_____ ☐
_____ ☐
_____ ☐

_____ ☐
_____ ☐
_____ ☐
_____ ☐
_____ ☐
_____ ☐

_____ ☐
_____ ☐
_____ ☐
_____ ☐
_____ ☐
_____ ☐

Notes

November

Monthly Focus

Special Dates

_____ _____
_____ _____
_____ _____
_____ _____
_____ _____

Home Keeping Tasks

☐ _____
☐ _____
☐ _____
☐ _____
☐ _____
☐ _____
☐ _____

Goals for the Month

_____ ☐
_____ ☐
_____ ☐
_____ ☐
_____ ☐
_____ ☐

_____ ☐
_____ ☐
_____ ☐
_____ ☐
_____ ☐
_____ ☐

_____ ☐
_____ ☐
_____ ☐
_____ ☐
_____ ☐
_____ ☐

Notes

_____
_____
_____
_____
_____
_____
_____
_____
_____
_____
_____
_____
_____
_____
_____
_____
_____
_____
_____
_____
_____
_____
_____
_____
_____
_____
_____
_____

December

Monthly Focus

1 _____
2 _____
3 _____

Special Dates

_____
_____
_____
_____
_____

Home Keeping Tasks

☐ _____
☐ _____
☐ _____
☐ _____
☐ _____
☐ _____
☐ _____

Goals for the Month

_____ ☐
_____ ☐
_____ ☐
_____ ☐
_____ ☐
_____ ☐

_____ ☐
_____ ☐
_____ ☐
_____ ☐
_____ ☐
_____ ☐

_____ ☐
_____ ☐
_____ ☐
_____ ☐
_____ ☐
_____ ☐

Notes

Week 1

Monday

Tuesday

Wednesday

Thursday

Friday

Saturday

Sunday

Places to Go

- ○
- ○
- ○
- ○
- ○
- ○

People to See

- ○
- ○
- ○
- ○
- ○
- ○

Things to Do

- ○
- ○
- ○
- ○
- ○
- ○
- ○
- ○
- ○
- ○
- ○

Special Reminders

- ○
- ○
- ○
- ○
- ○
- ○
- ○

Week 2

Monday

Tuesday

Wednesday

Thursday

Friday

Saturday

Sunday

Places to Go

- ○
- ○
- ○
- ○
- ○
- ○

People to See

- ○
- ○
- ○
- ○
- ○
- ○

Things to Do

- ○
- ○
- ○
- ○
- ○
- ○
- ○
- ○
- ○
- ○
- ○
- ○

Special Reminders

- ○
- ○
- ○
- ○
- ○
- ○
- ○

Week 3

Monday

Tuesday

Wednesday

Thursday

Friday

Saturday

Sunday

Places to Go

People to See

Things to Do

Special Reminders

Week 4

Monday

Tuesday

Wednesday

Thursday

Friday

Saturday

Sunday

Places to Go
- ○
- ○
- ○
- ○
- ○
- ○

People to See
- ○
- ○
- ○
- ○
- ○
- ○

Things to Do
- ○
- ○
- ○
- ○
- ○
- ○
- ○
- ○
- ○
- ○
- ○
- ○

Special Reminders
- ○
- ○
- ○
- ○
- ○
- ○

Week 5

Monday

Tuesday

Wednesday

Thursday

Friday

Saturday

Sunday

Places to Go

People to See

Things to Do

Special Reminders

Week 6

Monday

Tuesday

Wednesday

Thursday

Friday

Saturday

Sunday

Places to Go

People to See

Things to Do

Special Reminders

Week 7

Monday

Tuesday

Wednesday

Thursday

Friday

Saturday

Sunday

Places to Go

People to See

Things to Do

Special Reminders

Week 8

Monday

Tuesday

Wednesday

Thursday

Friday

Saturday

Sunday

Places to Go

- ○
- ○
- ○
- ○
- ○
- ○

People to See

- ○
- ○
- ○
- ○
- ○
- ○

Things to Do

- ○
- ○
- ○
- ○
- ○
- ○
- ○
- ○
- ○
- ○
- ○
- ○

Special Reminders

- ○
- ○
- ○
- ○
- ○
- ○
- ○

Week 8

Monday

Tuesday

Wednesday

Thursday

Friday

Saturday

Sunday

Places to Go

-
-
-
-
-
-

People to See

-
-
-
-
-
-

Things to Do

-
-
-
-
-
-
-
-
-
-
-
-

Special Reminders

-
-
-
-
-
-
-

Week 9

Monday

Tuesday

Wednesday

Thursday

Friday

Saturday

Sunday

Places to Go
○
○
○
○
○
○

People to See
○
○
○
○
○
○

Things to Do
○
○
○
○
○
○
○
○
○
○
○
○

Special Reminders
○
○
○
○
○
○
○

Week 10

Monday

Tuesday

Wednesday

Thursday

Friday

Saturday

Sunday

Places to Go

People to See

Things to Do

Special Reminders

Week 11

Monday

Tuesday

Wednesday

Thursday

Friday

Saturday

Sunday

Places to Go

- ○
- ○
- ○
- ○
- ○
- ○

People to See

- ○
- ○
- ○
- ○
- ○
- ○

Things to Do

- ○
- ○
- ○
- ○
- ○
- ○
- ○
- ○
- ○
- ○
- ○
- ○

Special Reminders

- ○
- ○
- ○
- ○
- ○
- ○
- ○

Week 12

Monday

Tuesday

Wednesday

Thursday

Friday

Saturday

Sunday

Places to Go
- ○
- ○
- ○
- ○
- ○
- ○

People to See
- ○
- ○
- ○
- ○
- ○
- ○

Things to Do
- ○
- ○
- ○
- ○
- ○
- ○
- ○
- ○
- ○
- ○
- ○
- ○

Special Reminders
- ○
- ○
- ○
- ○
- ○
- ○

Week 13

Monday

Tuesday

Wednesday

Thursday

Friday

Saturday

Sunday

Places to Go
- ○
- ○
- ○
- ○
- ○
- ○

People to See
- ○
- ○
- ○
- ○
- ○
- ○

Things to Do
- ○
- ○
- ○
- ○
- ○
- ○
- ○
- ○
- ○
- ○
- ○
- ○

Special Reminders
- ○
- ○
- ○
- ○
- ○
- ○

Week 14

Monday

Tuesday

Wednesday

Thursday

Friday

Saturday

Sunday

Week 15

Monday

Tuesday

Wednesday

Thursday

Friday

Saturday

Sunday

Places to Go

○
○
○
○
○
○

People to See

○
○
○
○
○
○

Things to Do

○
○
○
○
○
○
○
○
○
○
○
○

Special Reminders

○
○
○
○
○
○
○

Week 16

Monday

Tuesday

Wednesday

Thursday

Friday

Saturday

Sunday

Places to Go

People to See

Things to Do

Special Reminders

Week 17

Monday

Tuesday

Wednesday

Thursday

Friday

Saturday

Sunday

Places to Go

People to See

Things to Do

Special Reminders

Week 18

Monday

Tuesday

Wednesday

Thursday

Friday

Saturday

Sunday

Places to Go

- ○
- ○
- ○
- ○
- ○
- ○

People to See

- ○
- ○
- ○
- ○
- ○
- ○

Things to Do

- ○
- ○
- ○
- ○
- ○
- ○
- ○
- ○
- ○
- ○
- ○
- ○

Special Reminders

- ○
- ○
- ○
- ○
- ○
- ○
- ○

Week 19

Monday

Tuesday

Wednesday

Thursday

Friday

Saturday

Sunday

Places to Go
○
○
○
○
○
○

People to See
○
○
○
○
○
○

Things to Do
○
○
○
○
○
○
○
○
○
○
○

Special Reminders
○
○
○
○
○
○

Week 20

Monday

Tuesday

Wednesday

Thursday

Friday

Saturday

Sunday

Places to Go

People to See

Things to Do

Special Reminders

Week 21

Monday

Tuesday

Wednesday

Thursday

Friday

Saturday

Sunday

Places to Go

- ◯
- ◯
- ◯
- ◯
- ◯
- ◯

People to See

- ◯
- ◯
- ◯
- ◯
- ◯
- ◯

Things to Do

- ◯
- ◯
- ◯
- ◯
- ◯
- ◯
- ◯
- ◯
- ◯
- ◯
- ◯

Special Reminders

- ◯
- ◯
- ◯
- ◯
- ◯
- ◯
- ◯

Week 22

Monday

Tuesday

Wednesday

Thursday

Friday

Saturday

Sunday

Places to Go
- ○
- ○
- ○
- ○
- ○
- ○

People to See
- ○
- ○
- ○
- ○
- ○
- ○

Things to Do
- ○
- ○
- ○
- ○
- ○
- ○
- ○
- ○
- ○
- ○
- ○
- ○

Special Reminders
- ○
- ○
- ○
- ○
- ○
- ○
- ○

Week 23

Monday

Tuesday

Wednesday

Thursday

Friday

Saturday

Sunday

Places to Go

People to See

Things to Do

Special Reminders

Week 24

Monday

Tuesday

Wednesday

Thursday

Friday

Saturday

Sunday

Places to Go

- ◯
- ◯
- ◯
- ◯
- ◯
- ◯

People to See

- ◯
- ◯
- ◯
- ◯
- ◯
- ◯

Things to Do

- ◯
- ◯
- ◯
- ◯
- ◯
- ◯
- ◯
- ◯
- ◯
- ◯
- ◯
- ◯

Special Reminders

- ◯
- ◯
- ◯
- ◯
- ◯
- ◯
- ◯

Week 25

Monday

Tuesday

Wednesday

Thursday

Friday

Saturday

Sunday

Places to Go

People to See

Things to Do

Special Reminders

Week 26

Monday

Tuesday

Wednesday

Thursday

Friday

Saturday

Sunday

Places to Go

People to See

Things to Do

Special Reminders

Week 27

Monday

Tuesday

Wednesday

Thursday

Friday

Saturday

Sunday

Places to Go

- ◯
- ◯
- ◯
- ◯
- ◯
- ◯

People to See

- ◯
- ◯
- ◯
- ◯
- ◯
- ◯

Things to Do

- ◯
- ◯
- ◯
- ◯
- ◯
- ◯
- ◯
- ◯
- ◯
- ◯
- ◯
- ◯

Special Reminders

- ◯
- ◯
- ◯
- ◯
- ◯
- ◯
- ◯

Week 28

Monday

Tuesday

Wednesday

Thursday

Friday

Saturday

Sunday

Places to Go

People to See

Things to Do

Special Reminders

Week 29

Monday

Tuesday

Wednesday

Thursday

Friday

Saturday

Sunday

Places to Go

- ○
- ○
- ○
- ○
- ○
- ○

People to See

- ○
- ○
- ○
- ○
- ○
- ○

Things to Do

- ○
- ○
- ○
- ○
- ○
- ○
- ○
- ○
- ○
- ○
- ○
- ○

Special Reminders

- ○
- ○
- ○
- ○
- ○
- ○
- ○

Week 30

Monday

Tuesday

Wednesday

Thursday

Friday

Saturday

Sunday

Places to Go

- ◯
- ◯
- ◯
- ◯
- ◯
- ◯

People to See

- ◯
- ◯
- ◯
- ◯
- ◯
- ◯

Things to Do

- ◯
- ◯
- ◯
- ◯
- ◯
- ◯
- ◯
- ◯
- ◯
- ◯
- ◯
- ◯

Special Reminders

- ◯
- ◯
- ◯
- ◯
- ◯
- ◯

Week 31

Monday

Tuesday

Wednesday

Thursday

Friday

Saturday

Sunday

Places to Go

People to See

Things to Do

Special Reminders

Week 32

Monday

Tuesday

Wednesday

Thursday

Friday

Saturday

Sunday

Places to Go

People to See

Things to Do

Special Reminders

Week 33

Monday

Tuesday

Wednesday

Thursday

Friday

Saturday

Sunday

Places to Go
- ○
- ○
- ○
- ○
- ○
- ○

People to See
- ○
- ○
- ○
- ○
- ○
- ○

Things to Do
- ○
- ○
- ○
- ○
- ○
- ○
- ○
- ○
- ○
- ○
- ○
- ○

Special Reminders
- ○
- ○
- ○
- ○
- ○
- ○

Week 34

Monday

Tuesday

Wednesday

Thursday

Friday

Saturday

Sunday

Places to Go

-
-
-
-
-
-

People to See

-
-
-
-
-
-

Things to Do

-
-
-
-
-
-
-
-
-
-
-
-

Special Reminders

-
-
-
-
-
-
-

Week 35

Monday

Tuesday

Wednesday

Thursday

Friday

Saturday

Sunday

Places to Go

○
○
○
○
○
○

People to See

○
○
○
○
○
○

Things to Do

○
○
○
○
○
○
○
○
○
○
○
○

Special Reminders

○
○
○
○
○
○
○

Week 36

Monday

Tuesday

Wednesday

Thursday

Friday

Saturday

Sunday

Places to Go

People to See

Things to Do

Special Reminders

Week 37

Monday

Tuesday

Wednesday

Thursday

Friday

Saturday

Sunday

Places to Go
- ○
- ○
- ○
- ○
- ○
- ○

People to See
- ○
- ○
- ○
- ○
- ○
- ○

Things to Do
- ○
- ○
- ○
- ○
- ○
- ○
- ○
- ○
- ○
- ○
- ○
- ○

Special Reminders
- ○
- ○
- ○
- ○
- ○
- ○

Week 38

Monday

Tuesday

Wednesday

Thursday

Friday

Saturday

Sunday

Places to Go

People to See

Things to Do

Special Reminders

Week 39

Monday

Tuesday

Wednesday

Thursday

Friday

Saturday

Sunday

Places to Go
-
-
-
-
-
-

People to See
-
-
-
-
-
-

Things to Do
-
-
-
-
-
-
-
-
-
-
-
-

Special Reminders
-
-
-
-
-
-
-

Week 40

Monday

Tuesday

Wednesday

Thursday

Friday

Saturday

Sunday

Places to Go
- ○
- ○
- ○
- ○
- ○
- ○

People to See
- ○
- ○
- ○
- ○
- ○
- ○

Things to Do
- ○
- ○
- ○
- ○
- ○
- ○
- ○
- ○
- ○
- ○
- ○

Special Reminders
- ○
- ○
- ○
- ○
- ○
- ○

Week 41

Monday

Tuesday

Wednesday

Thursday

Friday

Saturday

Sunday

Places to Go

- ○
- ○
- ○
- ○
- ○
- ○

People to See

- ○
- ○
- ○
- ○
- ○
- ○

Things to Do

- ○
- ○
- ○
- ○
- ○
- ○
- ○
- ○
- ○
- ○
- ○
- ○

Special Reminders

- ○
- ○
- ○
- ○
- ○
- ○

Week 42

Monday

Tuesday

Wednesday

Thursday

Friday

Saturday

Sunday

Places to Go

-
-
-
-
-
-
-

People to See

-
-
-
-
-
-
-

Things to Do

-
-
-
-
-
-
-
-
-
-
-
-
-

Special Reminders

-
-
-
-
-
-
-

Week 43

Monday

Tuesday

Wednesday

Thursday

Friday

Saturday

Sunday

Places to Go

○
○
○
○
○
○

People to See

○
○
○
○
○
○

Things to Do

○
○
○
○
○
○
○
○
○
○
○
○

Special Reminders

○
○
○
○
○
○

Week 44

Monday

Tuesday

Wednesday

Thursday

Friday

Saturday

Sunday

Places to Go

People to See

Things to Do

Special Reminders

Week 45

Monday

Tuesday

Wednesday

Thursday

Friday

Saturday

Sunday

Places to Go

-
-
-
-
-
-

People to See

-
-
-
-
-
-

Things to Do

-
-
-
-
-
-
-
-
-
-
-
-

Special Reminders

-
-
-
-
-
-
-

Week 46

Monday

Tuesday

Wednesday

Thursday

Friday

Saturday

Sunday

Places to Go

-
-
-
-
-
-

People to See

-
-
-
-
-
-

Things to Do

-
-
-
-
-
-
-
-
-
-
-
-
-

Special Reminders

-
-
-
-
-
-
-

Week 47

Monday

Tuesday

Wednesday

Thursday

Friday

Saturday

Sunday

Places to Go

People to See

Things to Do

Special Reminders

Week 48

Monday

Tuesday

Wednesday

Thursday

Friday

Saturday

Sunday

Places to Go

People to See

Things to Do

Special Reminders

Week 49

Monday

Tuesday

Wednesday

Thursday

Friday

Saturday

Sunday

Places to Go
- ○
- ○
- ○
- ○
- ○
- ○

People to See
- ○
- ○
- ○
- ○
- ○
- ○

Things to Do
- ○
- ○
- ○
- ○
- ○
- ○
- ○
- ○
- ○
- ○
- ○
- ○

Special Reminders
- ○
- ○
- ○
- ○
- ○
- ○

Week 50

Monday

Tuesday

Wednesday

Thursday

Friday

Saturday

Sunday

Places to Go

People to See

Things to Do

Special Reminders

Week 51

Monday

Tuesday

Wednesday

Thursday

Friday

Saturday

Sunday

Places to Go

People to See

Things to Do

Special Reminders

Week 52

Monday

Tuesday

Wednesday

Thursday

Friday

Saturday

Sunday

Places to Go
-
-
-
-
-
-

People to See
-
-
-
-
-
-

Things to Do
-
-
-
-
-
-
-
-
-
-
-
-
-

Special Reminders
-
-
-
-
-
-
-

Week 53

Monday

Tuesday

Wednesday

Thursday

Friday

Saturday

Sunday

Places to Go

People to See

Things to Do

Special Reminders

My Personal Goals

This format will help you clarify your long-term goals. Be specific when listing goals, include at least 3 actions needed in order to achieve your goals, and don't forget a due date to ensure you take action. Keep this list in a place where you will see it each day; it will really help you stay focused on what's most important to you!

MY GOALS	ACTION STEPS	DUE DATE
LONG TERM		
	1.	
	2.	
	3.	
	1.	
	2.	
	3.	
SHORT TERM		
	1.	
	2.	
	3.	
	1.	
	2.	
	3.	
NOW		
	1.	
	2.	
	3.	
	1.	
	2.	
	3.	

My Personal Goals

This format will help you clarify your long-term goals. Be specific when listing goals, include at least 3 actions needed in order to achieve your goals, and don't forget a due date to ensure you take action. Keep this list in a place where you will see it each day; it will really help you stay focused on what's most important to you!

MY GOALS	ACTION STEPS	DUE DATE
LONG TERM	1.	
	2.	
	3.	
	1.	
	2.	
	3.	
SHORT TERM	1.	
	2.	
	3.	
	1.	
	2.	
	3.	
NOW	1.	
	2.	
	3.	
	1.	
	2.	
	3.	

Vacation Planning

DATES:

LOCATION:

BUDGET:

GETTING THERE

CAR RENTAL

LODGING

WHAT TO PACK

RECOMMENDED SIGHTS/RESTAURANTS

ITINERARY

NOTES:

Packing List

THE ESSENTIALS

- ○ Tickets
- ○ Passports
- ○ Car Rental Info
- ○ Itinerary
- ○ Reservation Info
- ○ Cell Phone Charger
- ○ Car Cell Phone Charger
- ○ Foreign Currency
- ○ Wallet/Purse
- ○ Medications

CLOTHING

- ○ Undergarments/Socks
- ○ Shirts/Blouses
- ○ Jeans/Pants/Shorts
- ○ Sweaters
- ○ Dresses/Skirts
- ○ Jacket
- ○ Pajamas/Robe/Slippers
- ○ Shoes/Sneakers
- ○ Workout Clothing
- ○

TOILETRIES

- ○ Shampoo/Conditioner
- ○ Cleansers/Soap
- ○ Toothbrush/Toothpaste/Floss
- ○ Cosmetics
- ○ Deodorant
- ○ Lip Balm
- ○ Brush/Comb
- ○ Razor/Shaving Cream
- ○ Contact Lens Solution

MISCELLANEOUS

- ○ Jewelry/Watch
- ○ Hairdryer
- ○ Camera/Video Camera
- ○ Memory Cards
- ○ Glasses/Sunglasses
- ○ Travel Guidebooks
- ○ Travel Journal
- ○ Books/Magazines
- ○ First Aid Kit
- ○ Antibacterial Wipes/Lotion
- ○ Stain Removal Wipes

FOR THE KIDS

- ○ Stroller
- ○ Diapers/Wipes/Changing
- ○ Pad
- ○ Diaper Bag
- ○ Food/Formula
- ○ Bottles
- ○ Sippy Cups
- ○ Utensils
- ○ Bibs
- ○ Medicines
- ○ Toys/Games
- ○ Stuffed Animal
- ○ Blanket
- ○ Books
- ○ Activity Books
- ○ Handheld Games
- ○
- ○
- ○
- ○

SKI ESSENTIALS

- ○ Waterproof Ski Jacket/Pants
- ○ Long Underwear
- ○ Skis/Boots/Poles
- ○ Ski Helmet
- ○ Goggles
- ○ Ski Gloves
- ○ Neck Warmer
- ○ Hat/Headband
- ○ Ski Socks
- ○ Hand/Foot Warmers
- ○ Turtlenecks/Extra Sweaters
- ○ Snow Boots
- ○ Ski Bag

BEACH ESSENTIALS

- ○ Swimsuit/Cover Up
- ○ Sunscreen/After-Sun Lotion
- ○ Beach Towels
- ○ Beach Chairs
- ○ Beach Umbrella
- ○ Goggles
- ○ Beach/Pool Toys
- ○ Sunhat
- ○ Sandals
- ○ Beach Bag

OTHER

- ○
- ○
- ○
- ○
- ○
- ○

Websites & Passwords

WEBSITE	USERNAME	PASSWORD

Websites & Passwords

WEBSITE	USERNAME	PASSWORD

Websites & Passwords

WEBSITE	USERNAME	PASSWORD

Websites & Passwords

WEBSITE	USERNAME	PASSWORD

Notes

Notes

Notes

Notes

Notes

Notes

Notes

Party Planning

DETAILS:

MENU

BEVERAGES

GUEST NAME

RSVP Y/N

Party Planning

DETAILS:

MENU

BEVERAGES

GUEST NAME

RSVP Y/N

Party Planning

DETAILS:

MENU

BEVERAGES

GUEST NAME

RSVP Y/N

Party Planning

DETAILS:

MENU

BEVERAGES

GUEST NAME

RSVP Y/N

Christmas Day Planner

GUEST NAME	# OF ADULTS	# OF KIDS	FOOD ITEM TO BRING

TOTAL # OF GUESTS _____

GROCERIES

APPETIZERS: _____

ENTREES: _____

SIDES: _____

DESSERTS: _____

BEVERAGES: _____

Grocery List

FRUITS
Apples
Bananas
Oranges
Lemons
Berries
Grapes
Melons

VEGETABLES
Lettuce
Spinach
Carrots
Onions
Garlic
Tomatoes
Cucumbers
Squash
Potatoes
Broccoli

MEAT
Beef
Chicken
Turkey
Fish
Seafood
Pork
Sausage
Hot Dogs
Hamburgers
Cold Cuts

DAIRY
Milk
Juice
Cheese
Butter
Eggs
Tortillas
Yogurt
Whipped Cream

PACKAGED
Chips
Cookies
Crackers
Popcorn
Pretzels
Nuts
Candy
Dips/Salsa
Fruit Cups
Energy Bars

BREADS
White
Wheat
Fresh Baked
Bagels
Muffins
English Muffins
Pita
Rolls
Donuts/Pastries

GRAINS
Pasta
Rice
Couscous
Dried Beans
Stuffing
Bread Crumbs

BREAKFAST FOOD
Oatmeal
Pancake Mix
Granola
Cereal Bars
Syrup
Cereals

BAKING GOODS
Baking Mixes
Flours
Sugars

CANNED
Soup
Broth
Tomatoes
Pasta Sauce
Beans
Tuna
Fruits
Vegetables

BEVERAGES
Soda
Beer/Wine
Energy Drinks
Juice
Water

MISCELLANEOUS
Ketchup
Mayonnaise
Salad Dressing
Peanut Butter
Jelly
Coffee
Tea
Oils
Vinegar
Salt
Pepper
Spices

FROZEN
Ice Cream
Waffles
Pizza
Fries
Bread
Meals
Snacks
Juice
Vegetables

HOUSEHOLD GOODS
Cleaning Products
Dish Liquid
Hand Soap
All-purpose
Bathroom
Floor/Carpet
Wood/Furniture
Glass/Window
Sponges
Trash Bags
Air Freshener
Hand Sanitizer
Miscellaneous

LAUNDRY
Detergent
Fabric Softener
Bleach
Starch
Stain Remover

PAPER PRODUCTS
Napkins
Paper Towels
Facial Tissue
Bathroom Tissue
Paper Plates
Paper Cups

MISC. HOUSEHOLD
Lunch Bags
Storage Bags
Storage Containers
Batteries
Coffee Filters

OTHER

Grocery List

FRUITS
Apples
Bananas
Oranges
Lemons
Berries
Grapes
Melons

VEGETABLES
Lettuce
Spinach
Carrots
Onions
Garlic
Tomatoes
Cucumbers
Squash
Potatoes
Broccoli

MEAT
Beef
Chicken
Turkey
Fish
Seafood
Pork
Sausage
Hot Dogs
Hamburgers
Cold Cuts

DAIRY
Milk
Juice
Cheese
Butter
Eggs
Tortillas
Yogurt
Whipped Cream

PACKAGED
Chips
Cookies
Crackers
Popcorn
Pretzels
Nuts
Candy
Dips/Salsa
Fruit Cups
Energy Bars

BREADS
White
Wheat
Fresh Baked
Bagels
Muffins
English Muffins
Pita
Rolls
Donuts/Pastries

GRAINS
Pasta
Rice
Couscous
Dried Beans
Stuffing
Bread Crumbs

BREAKFAST FOOD
Oatmeal
Pancake Mix
Granola
Cereal Bars
Syrup
Cereals

BAKING GOODS
Baking Mixes
Flours
Sugars

CANNED
Soup
Broth
Tomatoes
Pasta Sauce
Beans
Tuna
Fruits
Vegetables

BEVERAGES
Soda
Beer/Wine
Energy Drinks
Juice
Water

MISCELLANEOUS
Ketchup
Mayonnaise
Salad Dressing
Peanut Butter
Jelly
Coffee
Tea
Oils
Vinegar
Salt
Pepper
Spices

FROZEN
Ice Cream
Waffles
Pizza
Fries
Bread
Meals
Snacks
Juice
Vegetables

HOUSEHOLD GOODS
Cleaning Products
Dish Liquid
Hand Soap
All-purpose
Bathroom
Floor/Carpet
Wood/Furniture
Glass/Window
Sponges
Trash Bags
Air Freshener
Hand Sanitizer
Miscellaneous

LAUNDRY
Detergent
Fabric Softener
Bleach
Starch
Stain Remover

PAPER PRODUCTS
Napkins
Paper Towels
Facial Tissue
Bathroom Tissue
Paper Plates
Paper Cups

MISC. HOUSEHOLD
Lunch Bags
Storage Bags
Storage Containers
Batteries
Coffee Filters

OTHER

Grocery List

FRUITS
Apples
Bananas
Oranges
Lemons
Berries
Grapes
Melons

VEGETABLES
Lettuce
Spinach
Carrots
Onions
Garlic
Tomatoes
Cucumbers
Squash
Potatoes
Broccoli

MEAT
Beef
Chicken
Turkey
Fish
Seafood
Pork
Sausage
Hot Dogs
Hamburgers
Cold Cuts

DAIRY
Milk
Juice
Cheese
Butter
Eggs
Tortillas
Yogurt
Whipped Cream

PACKAGED
Chips
Cookies
Crackers
Popcorn
Pretzels
Nuts
Candy
Dips/Salsa
Fruit Cups
Energy Bars

BREADS
White
Wheat
Fresh Baked
Bagels
Muffins
English Muffins
Pita
Rolls
Donuts/Pastries

GRAINS
Pasta
Rice
Couscous
Dried Beans
Stuffing
Bread Crumbs

BREAKFAST FOOD
Oatmeal
Pancake Mix
Granola
Cereal Bars
Syrup
Cereals

BAKING GOODS
Baking Mixes
Flours
Sugars

CANNED
Soup
Broth
Tomatoes
Pasta Sauce
Beans
Tuna
Fruits
Vegetables

BEVERAGES
Soda
Beer/Wine
Energy Drinks
Juice
Water

MISCELLANEOUS
Ketchup
Mayonnaise
Salad Dressing
Peanut Butter
Jelly
Coffee
Tea
Oils
Vinegar
Salt
Pepper
Spices

FROZEN
Ice Cream
Waffles
Pizza
Fries
Bread
Meals
Snacks
Juice
Vegetables

HOUSEHOLD GOODS
Cleaning Products
Dish Liquid
Hand Soap
All-purpose
Bathroom
Floor/Carpet
Wood/Furniture
Glass/Window
Sponges
Trash Bags
Air Freshener
Hand Sanitizer
Miscellaneous

LAUNDRY
Detergent
Fabric Softener
Bleach
Starch
Stain Remover

PAPER PRODUCTS
Napkins
Paper Towels
Facial Tissue
Bathroom Tissue
Paper Plates
Paper Cups

MISC. HOUSEHOLD
Lunch Bags
Storage Bags
Storage Containers
Batteries
Coffee Filters

OTHER

Grocery List

FRUITS
Apples
Bananas
Oranges
Lemons
Berries
Grapes
Melons

VEGETABLES
Lettuce
Spinach
Carrots
Onions
Garlic
Tomatoes
Cucumbers
Squash
Potatoes
Broccoli

MEAT
Beef
Chicken
Turkey
Fish
Seafood
Pork
Sausage
Hot Dogs
Hamburgers
Cold Cuts

DAIRY
Milk
Juice
Cheese
Butter
Eggs
Tortillas
Yogurt
Whipped Cream

PACKAGED
Chips
Cookies
Crackers
Popcorn
Pretzels
Nuts
Candy
Dips/Salsa
Fruit Cups
Energy Bars

BREADS
White
Wheat
Fresh Baked
Bagels
Muffins
English Muffins
Pita
Rolls
Donuts/Pastries

GRAINS
Pasta
Rice
Couscous
Dried Beans
Stuffing
Bread Crumbs

BREAKFAST FOOD
Oatmeal
Pancake Mix
Granola
Cereal Bars
Syrup
Cereals

BAKING GOODS
Baking Mixes
Flours
Sugars

CANNED
Soup
Broth
Tomatoes
Pasta Sauce
Beans
Tuna
Fruits
Vegetables

BEVERAGES
Soda
Beer/Wine
Energy Drinks
Juice
Water

MISCELLANEOUS
Ketchup
Mayonnaise
Salad Dressing
Peanut Butter
Jelly
Coffee
Tea
Oils
Vinegar
Salt
Pepper
Spices

FROZEN
Ice Cream
Waffles
Pizza
Fries
Bread
Meals
Snacks
Juice
Vegetables

HOUSEHOLD GOODS
Cleaning Products
Dish Liquid
Hand Soap
All-purpose
Bathroom
Floor/Carpet
Wood/Furniture
Glass/Window
Sponges
Trash Bags
Air Freshener
Hand Sanitizer
Miscellaneous

LAUNDRY
Detergent
Fabric Softener
Bleach
Starch
Stain Remover

PAPER PRODUCTS
Napkins
Paper Towels
Facial Tissue
Bathroom Tissue
Paper Plates
Paper Cups

MISC. HOUSEHOLD
Lunch Bags
Storage Bags
Storage Containers
Batteries
Coffee Filters

OTHER

Made in the USA
Coppell, TX
28 November 2021